Peter Lippman's One and Only Wacky Wordbook

Golden Press • New York
Western Publishing Company, Inc.
Racine, Wisconsin

Cont

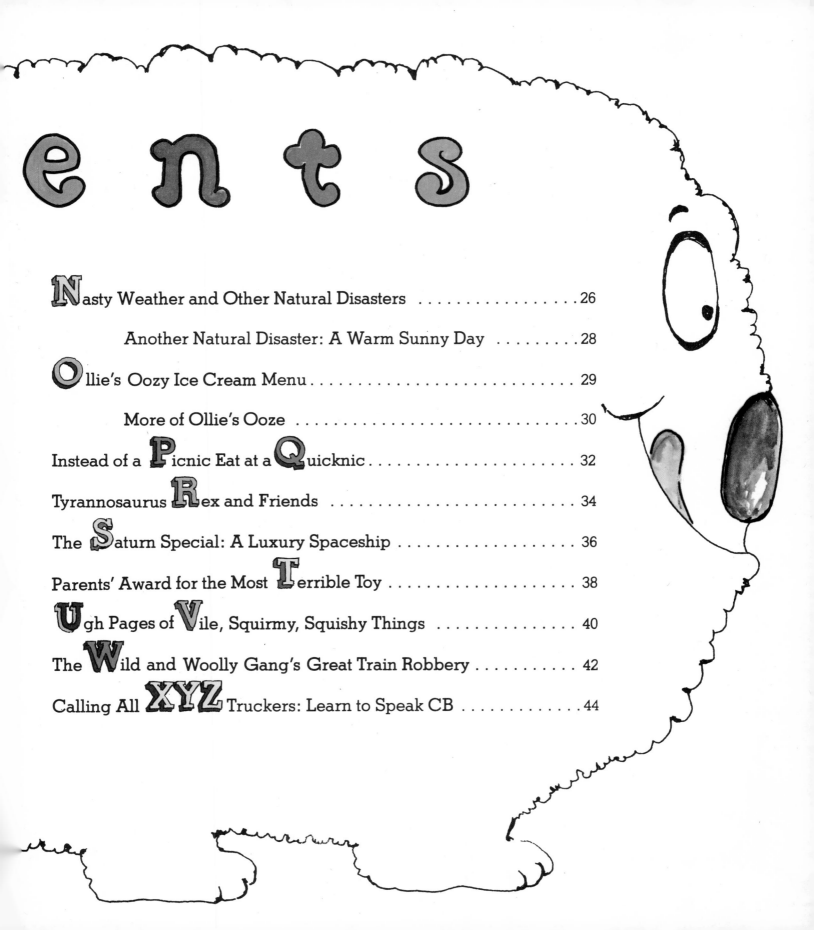

ents

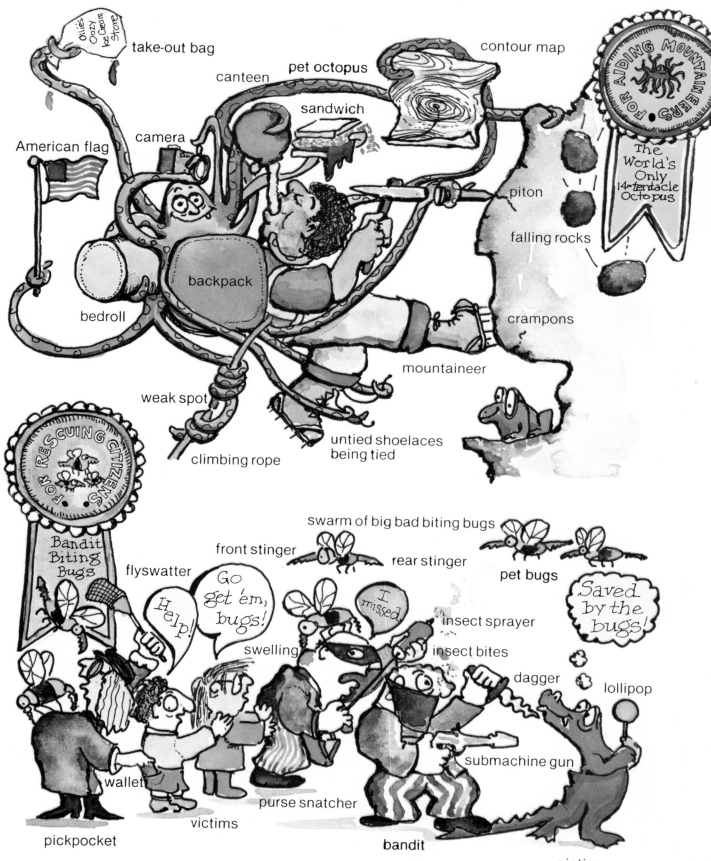

take-out bag

Ollies Oozy Ice Cream Store

canteen

pet octopus

sandwich

contour map

FOR AIDING MOUNTAINEERS

The World's Only 14-tentacle Octopus

camera

American flag

piton

falling rocks

backpack

bedroll

crampons

mountaineer

weak spot

untied shoelaces being tied

climbing rope

FOR RESCUING CITIZENS

Bandit Biting Bugs

swarm of big bad biting bugs

front stinger

rear stinger

pet bugs

flyswatter

Help!

Go get 'em, bugs!

I missed.

insect sprayer

Saved by the bugs!

swelling

insect bites

dagger

lollipop

wallet

submachine gun

purse snatcher

victims

pickpocket

bandit

victim

9

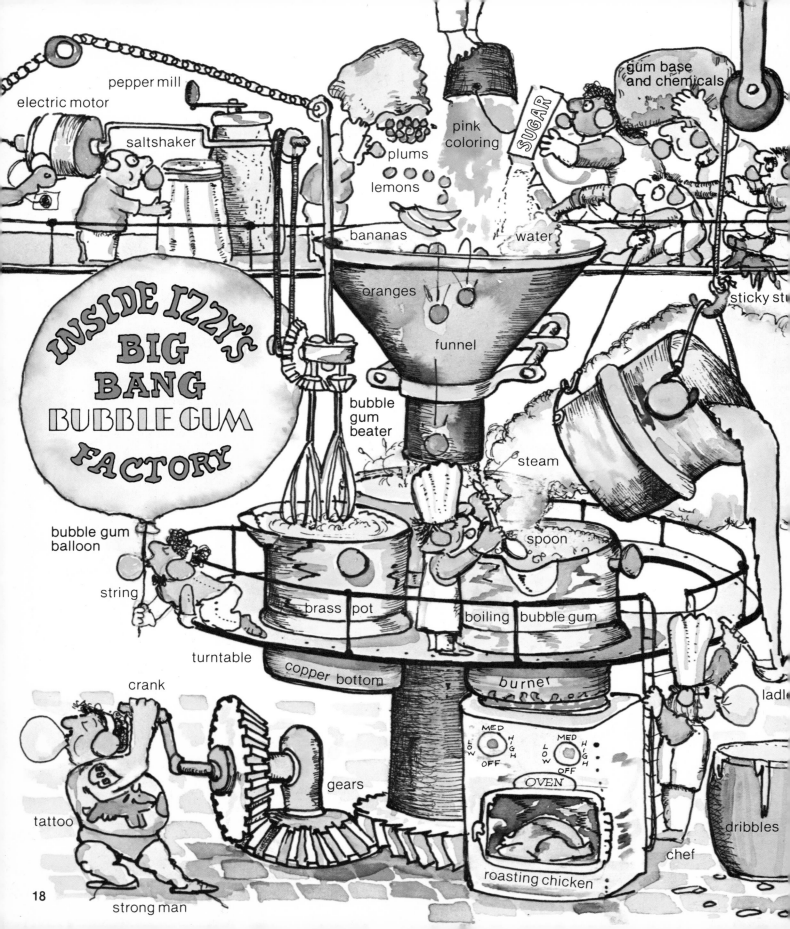

Nasty Weather and . . .

HAILSTORM — hailstones, leaf, broken stem, tomato

LIGHTNING STORM — thunder, Boom Boom, key, kite, lightning, Ben Franklin

TORNADO — house, foundation, trapdoor, front stoop, storm cellar

HURRICANE — power lines, high winds, fallen tree

FLOOD — streetlamp, RIVERSIDE DRIVE, roof, high water, rescuer

SANDSTORM — blowing sand, sand dune, tent, camel, desert

FOREST FIRE — spotter plane, ranger, trees, fire tower, bulldozer, fire fighters

FOG — foghorn, searchlight, lighthouse, ship, reef, buoy

...Other Natural Disasters

AVALANCHE

sliding snow

skier

Help

skier being buried

avalanche rope for rescuing the skier

TIDAL WAVE

foam

giant wave

tugboat

crew

captain

beach

EARTHQUAKE

collapsing building

cracking earth

howl

dog

OOWOO

VOLCANIC ERUPTION

smoke and ash

live volcano

extinct volcano

I like this one better.

molten lava

lava rock

DROUGHT

sun

dry riverbed

dead plants

dried mud

mirage

SODA

ROCK AND MUD SLIDE

boulder

mud

road

BLIZZARD

snowdrifts

snowflakes

snowbank

snowplow

27

Ollie's International Dishes

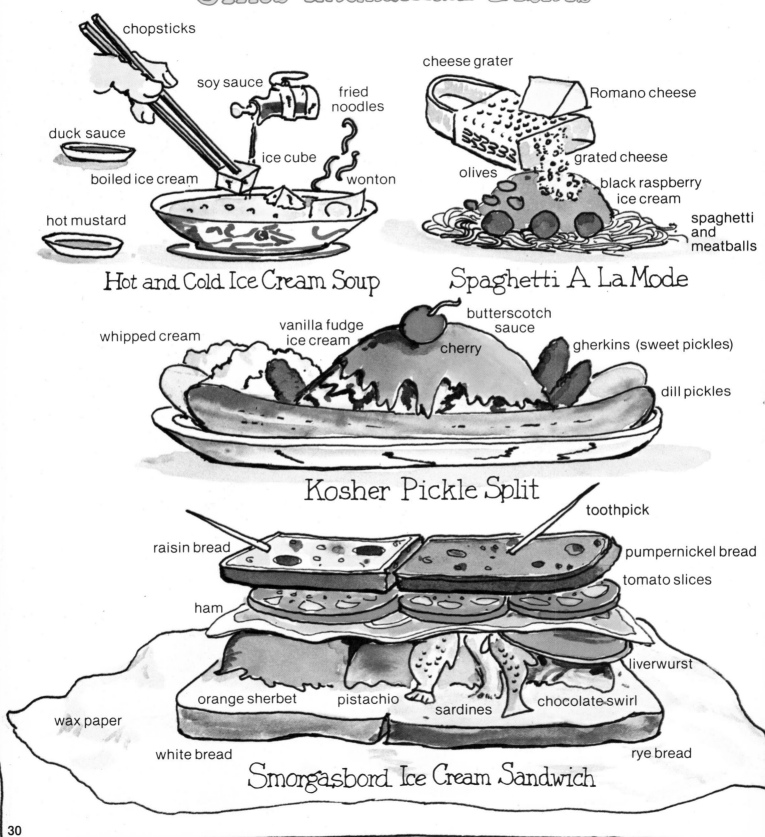

Hot and Cold Ice Cream Soup
- chopsticks
- soy sauce
- fried noodles
- duck sauce
- ice cube
- boiled ice cream
- wonton
- hot mustard

Spaghetti A La Mode
- cheese grater
- Romano cheese
- grated cheese
- olives
- black raspberry ice cream
- spaghetti and meatballs

Kosher Pickle Split
- whipped cream
- vanilla fudge ice cream
- butterscotch sauce
- cherry
- gherkins (sweet pickles)
- dill pickles

Smorgasbord Ice Cream Sandwich
- toothpick
- raisin bread
- pumpernickel bread
- tomato slices
- ham
- liverwurst
- orange sherbet
- pistachio
- sardines
- chocolate swirl
- wax paper
- white bread
- rye bread

Oozy American Dishes

waiter
ice cream scoop
customer
waitress
busboy
electric shaker
cash register
check-out counter

1 2 3

Three-Step Milk Shakes

Sunday Morning Breakfast Special
(Any Flavor Ice Cream – See Menu Cover)

pitcher
cream
asparagus ice cream
bacon
coffeepot
coffee
cold cereal
cream
sunny-side-up eggs
newspaper
grape jelly
French toast
sausages
syrup
comics

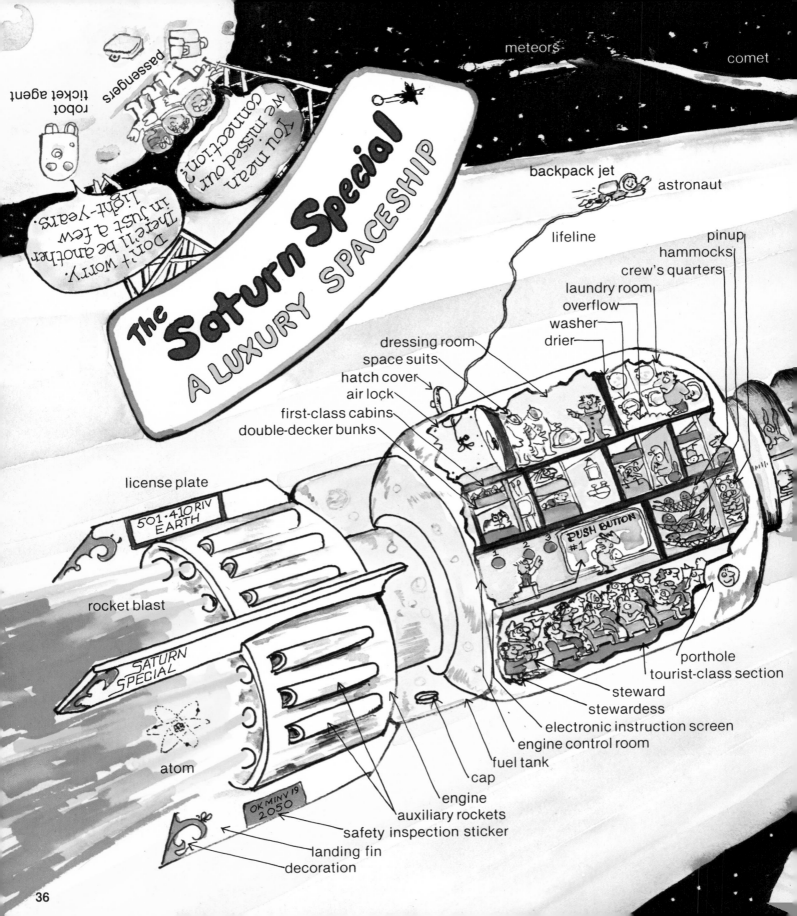

nebula

padded ceiling
padded walls
padded floor

no-gravity discotheque
free-floating guitar player
movie

command module
first mate
captain

nose cone

lounge

movie projector
wing nuts

navigator

stowaway
chandelier
column
switchboard

waiter
dining room
sauna
vista dome

lifeboat pods

flying saucers

stars

space pirate

space station

laser

constellation
(Big Dipper)

planet
moon

sun
solar system

asteroid lander

crater

space patrol

extraterrestrial

37

Ugh pages of Vile, Squirmy,

This is not my favorite page.

huge caterpillar

viper (a kind of snake)

an enemy

tomato sauce

green worms (baby caterpillars)

old, cold spaghetti

big brown cockroach

belly button

plain water-bug

bedbugs

big striped cockroach

sleeping person

fish guts

eel stew

pimple

thump thump

live clam

clamshell

maitre d'

scorpion

thump thump

tummy

melting tar